# *MY THREE WIVES*

## Lessons Learned On Choosing A Mate

*Perry  R. Whaley*

*&*

*Co-Author - Kelly Y. Ragin*

3G Publishing, Inc.
Loganville, Ga  30052
www.3gpublishinginc.com
Phone:  1-888-442-9637

First published by 3G Publishing, Inc.  October, 2020

ISBN:  9781941247839

Printed in the United States of America

# Contents

Dedication                                                              v

Acknowledgements                                                      vii

Introduction                                                           ix

Too Young To Know                                                      13

Just Because They're Good To You                                       19
Doesn't Mean They're Meant For You

Don't Force It - If It Doesn't Fit Keep it Moving                      25
Once The Ferris Wheel Stops

Choose Friendship, Love & Balance As a Firm                            31
Foundation

The Author                                                             33

Notes-to-Self                                                          35

# Dedication

I would like to dedicate my first book to my daughter Iyanna and my son, Brandon. They are my reason for going so hard. I want to continue proving to them that they can achieve anything that their hearts desire. The world is yours.

Anything.

# Acknowledgements

I  would first like to thank my higher power for all of my blessings throughout my journey.  Without Him I am nothing.

I would like to thank my life partner, Kelly for believing in me and assisting me with writing my personal story.

Also, a special thank you to my son, Brandon and my daughter Iyanna for supporting their Father on this journey.

I can never forget my parents-- Marie & Roosevelt who both gained their wings several years ago but are both still with me in my journey. I'm thankful for them bringing me into this world and pushing me to never give up.

To my 3 sisters.  I can never forget these ladies--Tracey, Christine and Marika, my beautiful sisters who have supported me along my journey.

I don't want to forget my brother Forrest and my entire Whaley family for their love and support.

May God continue to bless my journey.

-Perry

# Introduction

Preparation is everything.

I want to first thank God for my many opportunities and energy- because I know that energy breeds success. I've been telling myself this same message every day for quite a few years now. And guess what? It still holds true today. Energy and Opportunity certainly breeds SUCCESS! I'm a living witness. I awake each morning with more energy than the average person. I thank God daily for my measure of NEW MERCIES that I receive every day!

Writing this book was never anything that I set out to do. But sometimes, opportunities come along only once in a lifetime and that's when you have to grab it and make it happen!

I certainly appreciate this opportunity to share a small part of my story. Like so many others, I have always wanted to just enjoy the gift from the fruit of Love. I started at a very young age, learning very early about the joys of falling in love to the woes of having a broken heart. But even through my very own personal journey, no one could have ever prepared me for my journey of having a total of THREE WIVES.

This book is not about negativity or bad memories. In life, we all experience ups and downs—but it's what you make of it.

I will never take for granted my path. It's the one thing that made me who I am today. Good and bad. Great, and not so great. But---it's what made me.

My hope is that when you read my story, you will be inspired. That you will use these simple lessons learned to help you achieve better understanding and to make wiser choices in your love-life and ..........well, in your LIFE.

## Co-Author's Notes

### Kelly Y. Ragin

It brings me great pleasure to partner with Perry on this personal project. Prior to making the decision to write this book, we spent many hours discussing our lessons learned from past marriages. Our hiccups. Our hurt and our pain. We can relate on so many levels when it comes to discussing the joys, ups and downs of love and relationships.

We chose to pursue this project after the light bulb practically hit us in the head. We knew immediately that it couldn't be a long dragged out situation. But one that needed to have the nail hit on the head. We both believe in transparency. We truly believe that transparency equates to HEALING.

I'm extremely humbled and grateful for the opportunity to share these pages with this new author. The fact that we've both experienced marriage 3 times was enough to make me stand at attention! I immediately knew that the messages, tips, sound and Godly advice would benefit so many people who are like us. Those who are on the journey of seeking love and acceptance. Perry's perspective sheds light on love, friendship, marriage and balance. I'm so excited to be a part of this project; to translate and articulate his story. It was truly an amazing journey!

Blessings to you Perry! I can't wait to see what God has in store for you on the next one!

It's an honor to serve along side of you as a "Life-changing Agent" sir.

*-Kelly*

# *Chapter One*
## Too Young to Know!

When I reflect on my life as a young man, I think about how I was raised to view boy/girl and man/woman relationships. I grew up with both of my parents. They were truly committed to each other and my siblings and I knew that no matter what disagreements or discord we witnessed; we knew that they were going to be together. We didn't have the perfect family, but it was perfect for us -- through thick and thin.

**School Daze**

School was not something that I was in love with. I was not your average student. But I made it through. I was not the academic success story, but I loved sports. I loved drama. I loved my peers. So, I made the best of my "school daze".

After graduation, I made a decision to go to college. I was accepted into Virginia State University (VSU). I couldn't believe it! I'm forever grateful for the helping hands that helped to pave the way for me. I now understand what it means when it's stated that IT TAKES A VILLAGE!

I knew right off that I wanted to major in public administration. Though school was not something I was in love with, I knew it would help me get to my next level at some point in my young adult life. Although sports was my thing in high school, college brought about a whole brand-new different view.

For me, college was an opportunity for me to live my life as I had always wanted. Of course, this included the young ladies, partying and doing whatever it was I wanted to do. In my mind, it basically meant that I didn't have to be accountable to anyone but myself. College was my time to shine and my time to live it up! It was never a dream of mine but more so an opportunity for me to have the lifestyle of a footloose and fancy-free college student.

However, who knew that within the 4 years of college that the ultimate outcome would be me finding a wife. Within 3 years of attending VSU, I met a young lady who caught my attention immediately. Little did I know that this would be the start of my three wives. While in this relationship, I tried to maintain it the best that I could while also being a student. A very challenging task.

As a young man I must admit, being in a relationship or shall I say a serious relationship was not as important to me. What was most important to me in all actuality was me moving on to the next entanglement (thanks Jayda) with another beautiful young lady. Keep in mind, I'm still a young man who had just been given wings to fly, but I had no manual-- so for me the sky was the limit.

So now, I'm in this 1-Sided serious relationship. Sadly, I was not on the same page because my desire for other women overshadowed my view. I believe that when you are between the ages of 18 on up to your mid 20's this is a challenge for many in that age range.

From the start, as a young man, I was never committed to the relationship. And by not being committed to the relationship it led to pain, frustration and betrayal. During that time, I never saw this in the same light because in my mind, I never had a true commitment to the relationship. After all, I was a young man who had just started or entered college life ready to mix and mingle.

Unfortunately, because I lacked responsibility, the young lady became pregnant. And this was the beginning of wife number one.

**Commitment**

As I mentioned earlier, my father, who was the oldest of his siblings, was the one person that I admired.

I truly looked up to my dad because he always showed true commitment to his family. This meant a great deal to me and my siblings. So, for me at the age of 19, becoming a father was not in the plan. However, coming from a family structure where there had always been a mother and father present, I felt that I had no choice but to honor her and our unborn son by marrying her.

*TOO YOUNG TO KNOW.* Not only is this the title of my 1st chapter but it's the real truth! At the age of 19, I had no idea what I was about to embark upon and that my life was definitely about to change.

We married before our son was born. With the help of our parents, we tried our best to have a normal life and to provide the best for our newborn son.

We were married for one year. During that time, I left school to take on a full-time job. My hope was to be committed to my new family. After months of being new parents we discovered that it was much more of a challenge than we had expected.

Then suddenly, we realized the truth about what our parents meant when they would say we were too young to truly be married and more or less to even be parents.

Let me be clear-- I adored my role of being a new father and a new husband and a responsible family man. This was by far my number one goal. I had grown up watching my own father be this very person, so I had a great example. Now it was my turn to do the work.

In a nutshell, I truly believe that age played a huge factor of the final results of this marriage. We were both very young and did not have a full understanding of what marriage truly means. Nor did we have the tools on how to really raise a child.

I would say to anyone who's contemplating on marrying at a young age to ask themselves...

### *"AM I TOO YOUNG TO KNOW?"*

## HERE ARE A FEW QUESTIONS TO ASK YOURSELF:

1. Are you truly ready for a committed relationship?

2. Are you financially secure? Do you have stable employment?

3. Are you ready to give up your youth and all that comes with it to raise a family?

4. Are you willing to sacrifice or put your goals and dreams on hold?

5. Are you ready to combine your life with someone else's?

6. Have you "sown your oats"? This is not to imply that as a young adult that you should have sex or have LOTS of sex. It's simply to imply or reiterate that MARRIAGE IS A COMMITMENT TO ONE PERSON. There's no room for dating multiple people. Though many marriages still exist even through infidelity, it can create a major strain on the marriage. It can create levels of distrust that are often hard to recover. If flirting with multiple people is your thing, think twice.

7. Will you be prepared if an unplanned pregnancy occurs?

8. What do you consider to be your role as a spouse? Are you really ready to fulfill this role?

9. If you are the overseer of your household, do you recognize the importance of insurance for your family? Health, Life and Automobile Insurances? Seems minor, but this is a major requirement for what it means to be "RESPONSIBLE".

10. Do you truly LOVE your partner? Or is it infatuation?

*Quotes to consider......*

1. I know we're too young, and it's still early to say this... but I hope you're the one!

2. Young love can still be real love.

# *Chapter Two*

## Just Because They're Good to You
### Doesn't Mean That they're Good for You

After my 1st marriage ended I enjoyed being a bachelor. One might even say that I certainly played the field and played it well. I had my share of being in many relationships and also many challenging relationships.

Ultimately, I met someone who showed kindness and other qualities that made me feel that she was good for me. I gained a true appreciation for her and we also became great friends. I was still a very young man in my 20's but thought I had a better handle on this relationship thing.

A lesson learned for me is that sometimes we get caught up in what feels good at the moment. There are so many other factors that determine a good relationship and especially at a young age.

In all retrospect, she was really good to me-- more so than good for me. And Vice Versa. Although the marriage did not work, we are still friends today and both agree to these sentiments.

Sometimes men fall into relationships where they feel indebted to the woman. In my situation, my indebtedness came because my 2nd wife was there for me when I experienced a very trying time in my life. I made a horrible choice as a young man that landed me a 10-year prison sentence. She sacrificed much of her life for at least 10 years to cater to my needs. I am forever grateful. No words can express my true appreciation for her devotion, dedication and commitment. And because of this, I felt obligated to at least hold onto the last piece of fabric of that marriage because she had been there greatly for me.

This was hard because I recognized that the marriage wasn't working but I still felt obligated to her because she had been so GOOD to me. Again—REPEAT…. just because someone is good to you doesn't mean that they are good for you; and vice versa. Sometimes, people will sugar coat the burned piece of toast. Listen! You can NOT cover that burnt toast for long! You will smell the burn and eventually see it too! If this truth is staring you in the face, this is the time to have a real conversation. It really is not fair to either person. The TRUTH WILL SET YOU FREE! Yes—it might sting a little, but the pain will subside if it's handled with care and treated properly.

## SHOWING APPRECIATION~*WITHOUT Giving A RING!*

Fellas, this is a mistake that many of us make. It is certainly OK for us to show appreciation without giving a ring. When you show more appreciation through material giving it confuses a woman because some women believe that gift giving equates to "He Loves Me". Be verrrrrry careful here. Tread very lightly. Interpretation is certainly in the eye, or hands of the beholder. So, how can you show appreciation without confusing the real issue? For starters:

1. Keep the conversation very casual. Make sure your words are not "syrupy".

2. When offering to make up for a kind gesture, let it be known loud and clear why you want to "Repay" the favor. Be very specific with expressing your gratitude. Keep it short and don't linger long.

3. Eliminate a lot of personal eye contact. Limit hugging and hand holding in the midst of showing physical gratitude. Be strictly verbal but limit the amount of time you spend.

4. Consider sending or mailing a "Thank you F-R-I-E-N-D" card. This helps with avoidance. You prove that you're not trying to avoid while keeping your physical distance at bay.

### MORE THAN JUST S-E-X!

Why should a potential relationship be more than just physical?

Know the difference between love and lust. Love carries more weight. But you knew that! You make decisions differently if you remember that you can jeopardize losing the very person that you claim you love. Lust is short lived. It may be fun for the moment, but "What Happens After the Ferris Wheel Stops Spinning?

Once the Ferris wheel stops, you have 2 options. Stay on and go for another ride! Or GET OFF THE RIDE! It's as simple as that. But in real life, these options still require a CONVERSATION. Be sure that your potential partner understands upfront if you are only seeking a fun ride, or a fun time. A ton of hurt can come from this situation if truth is not spoken.

Today, Men have more to offer than when I was 18. There are so many resources available—which leads to no excuses. We have to first teach our young men that women are more than a sex object. As a matter of fact, we must teach them that women ARE NOT SEX OBJECTS. I have a daughter, and 3 sisters. I'm very mindful of this. Often. I didn't always operate in this manner and I definitely have regrets.

What it boils down to is the fact that most people are hoping to find love. REAL LOVE. Some will go to great lengths to find it. Some people settle and close the door on what could be the best thing since sliced bread. People settle out of Fear—and potentially, could seriously miss out on the one person God ordained for his/her life.

**Intimacy isn't just sex.
It's communicating. Listening. Holding hands.
Enjoying each other's interest. Spending
quality time together and loving on each other.**
*(Unknown Author)*

**Here are 7 self-help questions and points to ask yourself or consider in knowing if a person is the "right one" for you:**

1. Did you pray and ask God to reveal it first?

2. Is the person genuinely happy to see you when you arrive?

3. You are accepted for who you are—and no one is trying to change you!

4. They actually FIT into your life and lifestyle with ease.

5. They comfort you when needed.

6. They push you forward toward your dreams.

7. They have their own boundaries; but also respect yours.

# *Chapter Three*

## Don't Force it, if it Doesn't Fit
## Keep it Moving Once the Ferris Wheel Stops

WOW! At 50 years old, you would think that commitment would have been something simple. But instead, there was a period of loneliness after having not been in a committed relationship for 2 years. Then again, at the age of 50, I convinced myself that I should have been ready for a new relationship. I figured at my age; I should now REALLY be ready. Little did I know, I still wasn't ready.

**FUN DOESN'T DETERMINE FATE.**

Being settled at the age of 50, I felt committed to "keeping the fun". By this I mean, I enjoyed the company of my new mate. There was always something fun to do. We had a great time together. We enjoyed great company. Great food. Great entertainment. Great "good times". However, the compatibility was in relation to the type of careers we both had. We both worked long hours which meant when we were off, we valued the free time to do something exciting. But the compatibility should have been based on so much more.

Being married felt like the right thing to do because there was great compassion in the relationship, which could have been mistaken for love. It's important to know the difference so that no parties are hurt. I am not in the business of hurting people. I'm genuinely a very compassionate person. However, at some point, people should learn to have compassion for themselves. I didn't always take into consideration my own thoughts and feelings.

When you care for someone, it's easy to become consumed with their personal situation. In my case, I cared deeply, but recognized that it was more important to discuss the white elephant on the table instead of not living in my truth. I would venture to believe that she felt the same as well.

It's also extremely important to define what "compatibility" really means for you.

**COMPATIBILITY:**
A feeling of like mindedness.
A state in which 2 things or people are able to exist without problems or conflict. [Source: Oxford Language Dictionary]

**Do opposites really attract?**
The importance of compatibility in a relationship makes a huge difference in the future of maintaining your relationship.

**How do you know if you are compatible with your mate? Here are 15 questions to ask yourself:**
[jot your notes down in the back of this book]

1. You never question your relationship or your love for your mate.

2. You know secrets about your partner that only you two know

3. You have no desire to change your mate

4. You have no concern when you spend time apart

5. You both have common interest and enjoy a lot of the same activities

6. You're not afraid to have disagreements with your partner

7. You both are excited to achieve solutions when needed

8. You desire to become better because of the support from your mate

9. You see a fulfilled life and future together

10. You are able to be 100% authentically Y-O-U when with your boo!

11. You are genuinely attracted to each other.

12. You desire to keep family peace on both sides

13. You strive to keep spice in the relationship

14. You don't hesitate to put in time to keep the relationship alive

15. You know your mate's family. You're excited to show off your love

*"In one lifetime you will love many times, but one love will burn your soul forever."*

## Lessons Learned on Keeping A Marriage Solid

### 1) Kiss Goodnight, But Rise to the Occasion.

We've all heard the same advice. Never go to bed angry. And I agree. Especially, if it's late. Trying to make a point and express yourself while tired or frustrated never usually works in your favor. It's not fair to you or your partner if you can't show up and give 100%. Another thought to consider is that sometimes when you "sleep on it", you could easily have a change of heart by the next morning.

### 2) Upon entering the sanctity of marriage, remember to dismiss the "D" word.

If you both agree from the beginning of the engagement period that you won't allow the subject of Divorce to invade your space, then you've immediately activated your soldiers. Your soldiers will help to cover and protect your marriage as long as both spouses are in unison. When there are disagreements that always end in "I want a divorce", this creates distrust and could damage the marriage. Couples should be able to have disagreements without fear that this threat is going to resurface again.

### 3) The little things make a huge difference

Stock the fridge with his/her favorite foods or beverages, make sure to wear that sharp outfit that's a head turner on date night, and always make time to tell your sweetheart how much he/she means to you. Don't keep score but pay attention to the balance of the relationship.

### 4) Enjoy the early years- despite lack of finances

If finances are tight, then make serious efforts to change your financial situation. Just don't allow it to ruin the love that brought you both together. Thing is, you'll look back on this part of your marriage with a great big grin and appreciation. The first few years, as you figure out who you both are is the fabric of your married life. Enjoy the journey. Lack of money should not be the detriment of the marriage, but should bring about great creativity, and opportunities for you both to have a great time discovering life together.

### 5) Love equals action!

Love requires movement. Words are cheap. Empty promises are empty and leaves no value. Mean exactly what you say…and do EXACTLY what you said you would do. There's nothing more disappointing than when a spouse doesn't keep his/her commitment. Marriage is beautiful and also challenging at times. This is when you dig your heels in deeper. Always make a little extra effort to give it all you've got!

## "I LOVE YOU" means..

*That I accept you for the person that you are, and that I don't wish to change you into someone else.*

*It means that I do not expect perfection from you, just as you don't expect perfection from me.*

*"I LOVE YOU" means...that I will love you and stand by you even through the worst of times. It means loving you when you are in a bad mood or too tired to do the things I want to do. It means loving you when you are down, not just when you're fun to be with.*

*-Deanne Laura Gilbert*

# *Chapter Four*

Choose
~Friendship, Love & Balance~
as a firm foundation.

Love is truly beautiful when two people are determined to do whatever it takes to make love last. Why is choosing friendship, love and balance important in a long-term relationship?

## *Friendship*

Being friends first allows 2 people to get to know who their partner really is… in their own skin. It allows each person to be themselves. This is an easy way to find out if you really like the person too! Many times, we fall for the physical person instead of the inner person. And it actually takes time to get to know the real person anyway. Perhaps, you might get a glimpse within 6 months. One thing for sure, one will never really know everything there is to know about any person. However, if good advice is shared along with sound and Godly counsel, lessons learned and wisdom from those who are experienced –you can't go too far left!

## Love

Love is the glue that holds the friendship together. It also molds the relationship through the good and hard times. But it must be solid. When you find both friendship and love in the same person, you have definitely hit the jackpot. But even if it doesn't happen in that order, friendships can be developed, but should be nurtured along the way like any other friendship. We've heard over and over that friendships are like flowers and must be cared for or they could wither and die. I strongly encourage that for sure.

## Balance

Balance is what allows us to be human. It allows us to be independent of our own dreams, our personal goals, and our own personal interest. But it leaves enough room for us to come together …as ONE.

Here is one of our favorite Love quotes. It's quite encouraging when reflecting on friendship, love and balance.

*"Love Doesn't make the world go round. Love is what makes the ride worthwhile."*

-Franklin P. Jones

# The Author

## Perry R. Whaley

### BIO

Mr. Perry Whaley was born in Brooklyn, NY and raised in Virginia Beach, Virginia. He attended Virginia State University where he majored in Public Administration. Today, he is the Founder of the Non-profit organization called, Vitiligo Man of Action. His organization helps raise awareness for the skin condition called Vitiligo and also provides Mentorship programs for youth who are struggling with the skin condition. He also offers mentorship to at risk youth boys as well. Perry has spent many years as one of Atlanta's top car salesmen over the last two decades. Today, his focus is merely on being a voice and an asset to the community.

**Empowering and Educating Individuals**

**Vitiligo Man of Action LLC** in Stonecrest, Georgia is committed to helping people better understand vitiligo, a disease in which areas of skin lose their normal pigmentation, resulting in white patches. One's hair, as well as other parts of the body, may also be affected by the lack of melanin.

His mission is to raise public awareness about this skin disorder and how it affects members of the community through education. In this way, individuals living with vitiligo will be able to live their best lives knowing that there are people who understand their condition.

We made it our mission to raise awareness about vitiligo, empower those whose lives are affected by it, and educate individuals who may be unaware of the skin condition. Ultimately, we want to influence the community to take action against social neglect and discrimination.

Speaking Engagement Portfolio
- FOX 5 News Atlanta, Georgia
- WCLK 91.9 Radio Atlanta, Georgia
- V-103 Radio Atlanta, Georgia
- Kiss 104 Radio Atlanta, Georgia
- Atlanta Live! Television
- Morehouse School of Medicine, Atlanta, GA
- J.E. Brown Middle School, Atlanta, Georgia
- Salem Middle School, Lithonia, Georgia
- Berean Baptist Church, Snellville, Georgia
- WYZE Radio, Alabama
- Houston, TX  (Vitiligo Awareness 30 City Tour)
- Black Caucus Convention (Vitiligo Awareness)
- Tuskegee University, Tuskegee, Alabama, Georgia
- Spark Plug Radio, People You Need to Know Business Guide

If you are interested in inviting Perry to speak at a future event, please connect via PerryWhaley136@gmail.com.

# *Notes-to-Self*

## Here are 15 questions to ask yourself:

### How do you know if you are compatible with your mate?

You never question your relationship or your love for your mate.  Do you feel truly loved?

You know secrets about your partner
that only you two know?
Do you feel that you're his/her confidante?

_____

_____

_____

_____

_____

_____

_____

_____

_____

_____

_____

_____

_____

_____

_____

_____

_____

_____

_____

_____

_____

_____

_____

_____

_____

You have no desire to change your mate.
Are you completely satisfied with the person you see and
spend time with on a regular basis?

_____

_____

_____

_____

_____

_____

_____

_____

_____

_____

_____

_____

_____

_____

_____

_____

_____

_____

_____

_____

_____

_____

_____

You have no concern when you spend time apart.
Do you secretly question his/her
whereabouts in your mind?
Are you at ease or unrest when you are not together?

_____

_____

_____

_____

_____

_____

_____

_____

_____

_____

_____

_____

_____

_____

_____

_____

_____

_____

_____

_____

_____

_____

_____

_____

_____

You both have common interest and enjoy
a lot of the same activities.

_____

_____

_____

_____

_____

_____

_____

_____

_____

_____

_____

_____

_____

_____

_____

_____

_____

_____

_____

_____

_____

_____

_____

_____

_____

You're not afraid to have disagreements
with your partner.

_____

_____

_____

_____

_____

_____

_____

_____

_____

_____

_____

_____

_____

_____

_____

_____

_____

_____

_____

_____

_____

_____

_____

_____

_____

You both are excited to achieve solutions when needed.

You desire to become better because
of the support from your mate.

You see a fulfilled life and future together.

_____
_____
_____
_____
_____
_____
_____
_____
_____
_____
_____
_____
_____
_____
_____
_____
_____
_____
_____
_____
_____
_____
_____
_____
_____
_____

You are able to be 100% authentically
Y-O-U when with your boo!

You are genuinely attracted to each other.

_____
_____
_____
_____
_____
_____
_____
_____
_____
_____
_____
_____
_____
_____
_____
_____
_____
_____
_____
_____
_____
_____
_____
_____

You desire to keep family peace on both sides.

You strive to keep spice in the relationship.

You don't hesitate to put in time to
keep the relationship alive.

You know your mate's family.
You're excited to show off your love.

One day Love met Friendship.

Love asked,
Why do you exist when
I already exist?

Friendship replied,
To put a smile where
you've left tears.

He's not my boyfriend.
But I love his smile, his eyes,
his kindness & all the times
we laughed together...
I guess I fell in love
with our
**friendShip** ♥